A
Candid
(& slightly sweary)
Guide to Piano
for
Adult Beginners.

by

L. Blake

Foreword.

If life has taught me one thing it's that patience is a finite commodity, and it seems my personal supply ran out some time around the time Azerbaijan won the Eurovision Song Contest.

I have been a music teacher for more than twenty years and in that time, I've heard it all; the stupid questions. The excuses. The general tapestry of bullshit that people weave in hopes of disguising their own laziness, and let me tell you, it wears a person down. Teaching for a living would be enough to make the Care Bears turn to fentanyl. As a result, this book is neither wholesome nor polite. It will not dance courteously around your inadequacies nor squeeze your hand to guide you through the rough times. It does not care about your feelings, so if you're a delicate little doily then I'd suggest you close this book right here, flog it at your next local car boot sale, and use the money to buy one of the more classic tutor books that won't have you clutching your pearls.

That being said...

Congratulations on buying (or on being gifted) this book. With this, you can take your first steps towards being the twinkle-fingered smart-arse you've always longed to be.

If you picked this book up from a second hand shop or bought it 'used but in good condition' from an online auction site, it could be that the previous owner finished it and has progressed to more advanced playing. Right now, as you're reading this, they might be at some swanky cocktail party in a penthouse apartment, casually playing smooth jazz on a baby grand whilst partygoers in slinky frocks bring them flutes of champagne and tell them how talented they are. Imagine that the seller of this book is that kid from school who ate egg sandwiches on the bus. That shit *stunk*. You can't let stinky-egg-kid be more successful than you.

Of course, it could well be that the seller didn't get past page two. It's all too easy to give up on things when they get difficult, isn't it? Just look at Napoleon.

So, sit yourself down at your piano or keyboard or Mellotron.

Your bellybutton should be around key-height. Your wrists should be slightly lifted, your fingers curved. Your little finger, wrist, and elbow should form a straight line. If you're short and your feet don't reach the ground, find something to rest them on, like a small stool, a stack of books, or Ron from next door.

FAQ:

"I'm no spring chicken anymore! How hard will it be for me to learn to play the piano?"

Think about all that binge-drinking you did in your early twenties, or the cheap coke you shovelled up your nose-holes in nightclub bathrooms. Perhaps you bashed your head one too many times playing that spin-around-the-broom-at-a-barbeque game. Maybe you like a good strangle-wank. All that stuff has repercussions. In the process of trying to scrape a tiny modicum of pleasure out of your adult life you've slowly been dissolving, rotting, and generally obliterating your brain of functioning neurons. It might be that those exact neurons are the ones you need in order to learn to play the piano. Probably. Who knows? Not me, I'm not a doctor.

"How long will it take for me to be able to play Mozart?"

Give me a second to check my crystal ball. Oh, that's right – I can't see into the future.
And you'll have to be more specific. If you're asking how long it will take you to play it *well*, then I'd say we'll have to wait and see. You might have a natural aptitude for it, and your coordination and understanding might be above average. Or you might flap about aimlessly like a pigeon in a jet engine and struggle to remember what a stave is.
Just about anyone can pick through the notes with no discernible grace, sense of pulse, or technique, so if that makes you feel more optimistic about all this, then good for you.

FAQ continued...

"I don't want to learn all the technical names for stuff, I just want to play tunes."

Oh, really? Well, I guess I'll just go build a skyscraper, then. I mean, I have no previous experience of building anything, but at the same time I can't be arsed to learn about construction materials, load-bearing structures, or safety codes. Fuck it. I just want a really tall, wobbly building that nobody will want to look at or use, and will collapse the first time someone farts near it. That's how you sound right now.

"How much practise will I need to do?"

Enough to see an improvement. It's not going to happen by magic. Think of other things you've accomplished in your life so far simply through repetitive practice:

- riding a bike

- driving a car

- stifling the constant urge to lose your shit completely, tell everyone around you to fuck off, drive to the airport, dump your phone in a bin, get on a last-minute flight to Mexico, drown yourself in cheap Tequila, and wake up naked in the desert with no passport, no wallet, and donkey hairs all over your clothes.

It doesn't happen without practise. So probably do, like, 20-45 minutes a day.

Absolute Basics.

Sit in front of your piano and look at the keys. The white ones use the letters of the alphabet from A to G in a seemingly endless loop. You'll need to be able to go through these in order, and also backwards. As we go to the RIGHT we move upwards, and the notes get higher in pitch. As we go LEFT, we move downwards, and the notes get lower in pitch.

etc F G **A B C D E F G** A B C D E etc

If we start by playing the A key, and move up step-by-step through the alphabet (along the white keys, one-by-one) until we reach the next A key, then we've played an **octave**.

The same goes for the other keys, too;

B to B = an octave.

C to C = an octave.

D to D ...well, you get the idea.

I hope so, anyway, because these are the absolute basics. If you don't understand this part then you may as well close this book, sell your piano, and take up something less cerebral, like swimming or politics.

Hands.

The first thing to establish is that you know your left from your right.

It might sound ridiculous, but you have no idea how many grown adults still get confused by this. If you're one of these people, I can only hope you don't drive a car.

From here on in, your fingers are numbered. Both thumbs are 1. Your little fingers are 5. You should be able to figure out the ones in between, and for those of you who can't, here's a diagram, you absolute wassock:

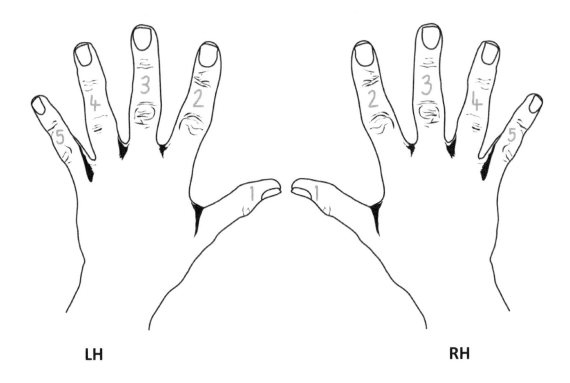

LH   RH

*If any of your fingers are missing on either hand, you're going to have to improvise somewhat. If *all* of your fingers are missing, then hat's off to you for choosing piano playing as your hobby. No, seriously. Brave choice.

Reading music.

You've got to learn to read music. Stop screwing your face up – you knew this before you started, and if you didn't then I bet you're one of the people who doesn't know their left from their right.

Below, you will see a STAVE. These are the lines on which music notes are written. The stave at the top will contain the notes which are to be played by your Right Hand. The stave at the bottom will contain the notes which are to be played by your Left Hand.

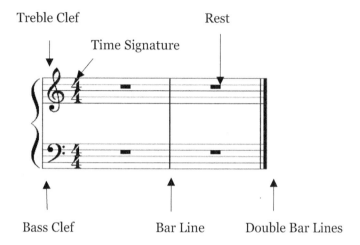

Clefs (Treble and Bass): These symbols indicate the pitch of the notes written on the stave. Don't stress about this, yet. There's plenty of time to stress about it later.

Time Signature: These numbers tell you how many beats each bar contains. The above time signature of 4/4 tells us that we are counting four beats in every bar.

Bar Lines: These lines are the dividers for the beats. Every 4/4 bar has to contain four beats in total, and the bar lines mark each of these sets of four.

Double Bar Lines: These two lines mark the end of the piece. It's over. Finished. Anyone listening to you is probably relieved about that.

Rests: When you see a rest, don't press any keys. Do nothing. Just like you do at work on a Friday afternoon.

Pitch.

Middle C in both clefs

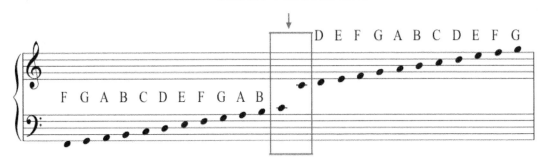

The further down the stave the note head is, the lower the note's sound. The higher up the stave, the higher the note's sound. The further right on the keyboard the notes are, the higher they sound. The further left, the lower they sound. Logical, eh?

Hopefully, you can see in the example that the music starts low, gradually moves higher and higher up the stave, and then gradually moves back down again, until it finishes on the same note that on which it began. If you *can't* see that, maybe it really is true that excessive masturbation sends you blind.

As the notes move up the stave, so too do they move up through the alphabet. Clearly this means that moving down through the stave means the alphabet runs backwards.

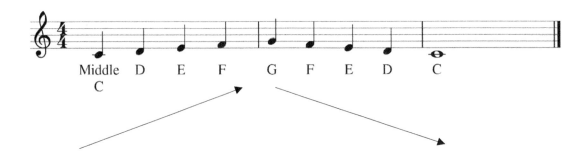

You may notice that some of the note heads are on the lines (ie. The line passes through the middle of it) and others sit in the spaces (between the lines.)

There are a few ways to remember the names of the middle-range notes, and one of those ways is with mnemonics.

Treble Clef:

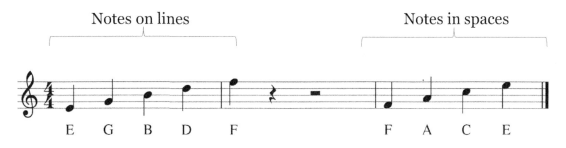

Lines: **Every** **Good** **Boy** **Deserves** **Fruit**

Spaces: **F**   **A**   **C**   **E**

Bass Clef:

Lines: **Grizzly** **Bears** **Don't** **Fear** **Anything**

Spaces: **All**   **Cows**   **Eat**   **Grass**

Note naming practice.

Fun Fact! Composer Robert Schumann treated his ailments by plunging his hands into the entrails of slaughtered animals.

Treble Clef – Right hand

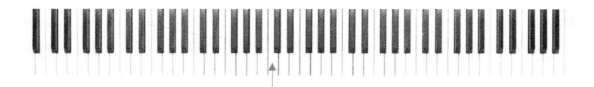

This is MIDDLE C.

With your RIGHT HAND, find your hand position:

1 on Middle C / 2 on D / 3 on E / 4 on F / 5 on G

Play the following pattern:

C D E F G F E D C

1 2 3 4 5 4 3 2 1

Now we're going to see how this would look written out 'properly', on a stave, because it's time you stopped being such an amateur, dammit. Look at this and play it. Go on.

If you managed to play it, then congratulations – you just read and played your first piece of music.

If you failed, then you have two options;

1. Keep trying until you get it right.

2. Give up like you always do, and when your friends and family ask you in a few weeks, 'so, how's the piano playing going?' you can whip up some shitty excuse like, 'oh, I just didn't have the time to fit in the practise' and then distract them with yet another boring story about a medical issue you've probably got.

Bass Clef – Left Hand

This is the C below Middle C

With your LEFT HAND, find your hand position:

5 on the C below Middle C / 4 on D / 3 on E / 2 on F / 1 on G

Starting with C, play the following pattern:

C D E F G F E D C

5 4 3 2 1 2 3 4 5

Let's see how it should look when it's written out on a stave:

Did you do it? Did you read the music? Did it sound okay? Are you feeling a rush of accomplishment? Is it starting to dawn on you that this is more complicated than you were anticipating? Do you kinda wish you'd just bought a bottle of wine and a lottery ticket instead of this book? Well tough titties. You bought it. See it through, and show your parents you're worthy of love after all.

Note & Rest Values.

Notes & rests last for a varying number of beats, and each one has its own name. Here are the first ones you need to know;

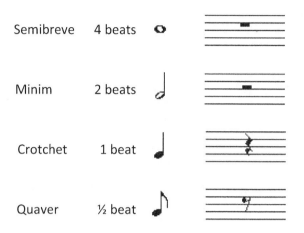

Semibreve	4 beats	
Minim	2 beats	
Crotchet	1 beat	
Quaver	½ beat	

The astute among you may have already sussed out that the tunes you just played with your right hand then left hand used some of these note values, and would have been counted like this:

Of course, the less astute may be sitting there, mouth slightly agape, wondering what the ever-loving heck is going on. Maybe it's time to take a break. Go get yourself a biscuit and text your friends about something arbitrary in an effort to avoid the reality of your own shortcomings.

Fun Fact! Soprano Dame Nellie Melba died of sepsis after a botched facelift operation.

Examples using rests.

As you play each one of these, imagine there's a ticking clock inside your skull. Keep the beat, even through the rests. Without a beat, the noise is incessant and has no meaning. If you've ever spent time with a toddler, you'll know how bloody irritating this is.

Right hand:

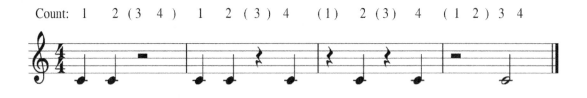

Left hand:

Dotted notes & rhythms.

A dot after a note means that the length of that note has been extended by half of its value.

$$\mathbf{o} \cdot = \mathbf{o} + \textsf{d}$$

$$\textsf{d} \cdot = \textsf{d} + \textsf{d}$$

$$\textsf{d} \cdot = \textsf{d} + \textsf{♪}$$

A common combination using dotted notes is this one  which fits perfectly to the rhythm we use when we say the word 'baby'.

Anoother common combination is this one  which fits perfectly to the rhythm we use when we say the word 'marmalade.'

Have a go at playing these dotted rhythms:

'Skye Boat Song'
Trad. Scottish

(tuck thumb under to G)

'Happy Birthday To You.'

15

Time Signatures.

At the beginning of every piece of music is a time signature. A time signature tells us how many beats are to be counted in every bar, so that you may demonstrate some semblance of rhythmic control.

(Not like that time you danced pissed at Janet's wedding and thought you could pull off those breakdancing moves but ended up spraining your wrist and vomiting down the flower girl's back. Janet said it was fine but you've noticed how distanced the two of you have become since then, which is a real shame because you used to have a right laugh together. You haven't heard from her in a while, have you? Maybe you should text her. Not now, though. You've got piano practice to do.)

There are two numbers in a time signature.

The top number tells you how many beats there are in each bar.

The bottom number tells you what kind of beats they are.

For example: **4** ◄——— Four beats in every bar
               4 ◄——— The beats are crotchets

Therefore: **4**
               4 = four crotchet beats per bar.

               3
               4 = three crotchet beats per bar

               2
               4 = two crotchet beats per bar

*Sometimes, in an example of laziness from olden hand-written times, the time signature 4/4 can be written simply as the letter C, which stands for 'common time.'

Fun Fact! Mozart wrote lots of poems about scat, including this one:
"Lick my arse nicely, lick it nice and clean…that's a greasy desire, nicely buttered."

Starting to Play Stuff.

Take a deep breath. Focus. Do you need to pee? Are you sure? We're not stopping halfway through because of your inability to plan ahead. Okay, then. We're about to put all the stuff from earlier into action.
Play these with your right hand. Begin with your thumb (1) on Middle C.

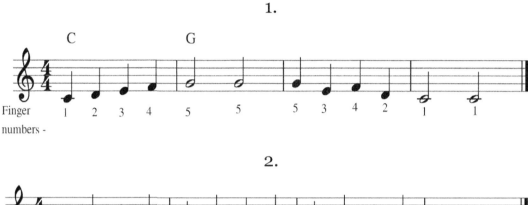

Now play these with your left hand. Begin with your little finger (5) on the C below Middle C. If you're right-handed this is going to feel a bit awkward, like that time someone younger and cooler tried to fist-bump you but thought they were going to go for a more traditional handshake so you ended up weirdly holding their knuckles instead.

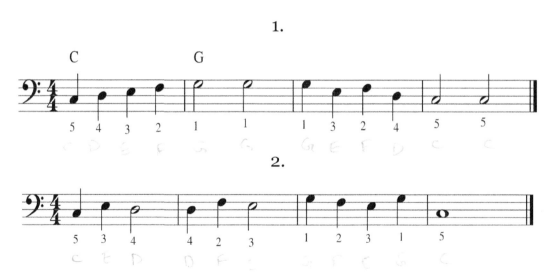

Okay, smart-arse, think you're ready to play both hands together at the same time? Give it a go.

What's the worst that can happen? You can't do it, which triggers flashbacks to the hundreds of other times you've failed in life, and so you decide to drink some wine to take the uncomfortable memories away, but it doesn't take them away, it only serves to magnify them and all you want to do now is to flee from the feelings of inadequacies that have plagued you your whole life, and there you go, getting into your car and driving drunk in an effort to clear your head but you're not thinking straight and you don't see that cyclist in time, you just don't see him, and there he goes, bouncing off your hood, and you know he might be dead but you can't stop to check because you're drunk driving and people like you don't do well in prison?

I mean, yeah, the worst that can happen is that maybe you'll fuck it up and trigger a terrible chain of events, but you don't have to go getting drunk and committing manslaughter. Just play it again until you get it right. Jeez. Drama queen or what?

1.

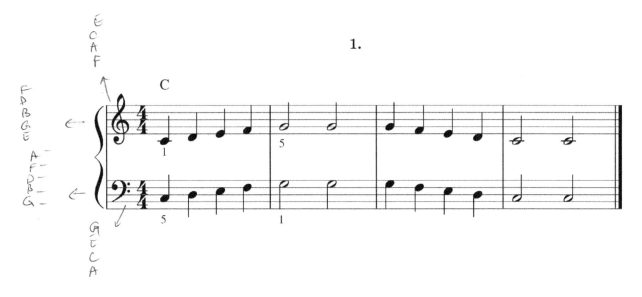

2.

18

'The Blue Danube'
J. Strauss

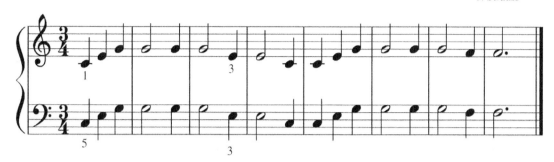

Those last ones were played in unison (meaning you were playing the same notes in your left and right hands at the same time.) Of course, this isn't always how it'll be. We want to create those sweet, sweet harmonies, which can be achieved by playing different notes in each hand.

Here you go. Give this a bash.

'Lightly Row'

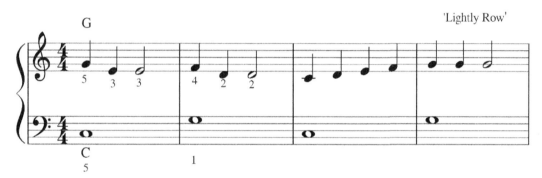

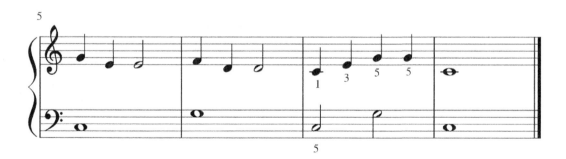

And now this one...

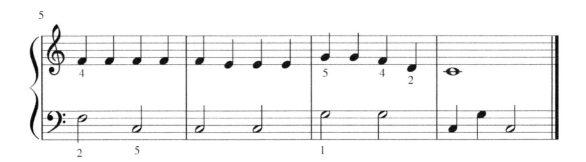

Why not play this one to the family on Christmas day? If you'll be spending the holiday season alone, maybe you could play this in the break between opening the gifts you bought yourself, and weeping into a glass of wine whilst watching the Queen's Speech.

And another...

Oh, and this one...

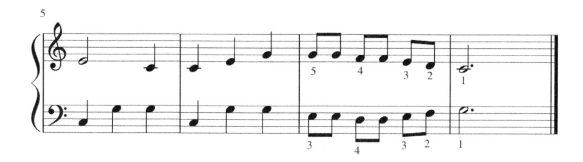

Accidentals
(sharps, flats, naturals.)

If you've ever overheard your parents arguing in the kitchen late at night after they've had a few sherries, you've likely heard them say that you were an 'accident' and that you 'ruined their lives.' In music, accidentals don't mean anything like that, so you can pop your trauma in your pocket and crack on with this.

The notes we've played so far have all been white keys, and our hand positions have always begun on the note of C. Clearly there are more notes on the piano, and in order to make sure the music we play isn't as dull as a tennis player's sock drawer, we have to start using them.
First, we have to know about tones and semitones.

A semitone is the smallest distance between two notes. This can be a white to a black key, a black to a white key, or even (in the cases of B to C, and E to F) a white key to another white key.

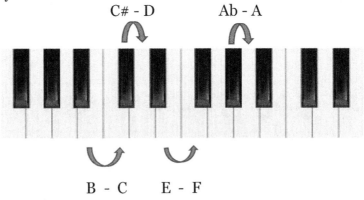

If there is a note between the two notes we're looking at, then they are a tone apart.

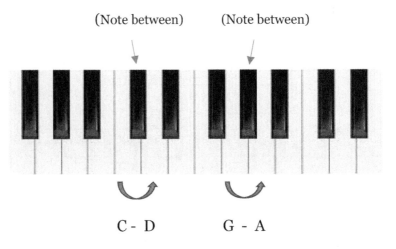

22

Sharps:

A sharp sign (#) is placed before a note on the stave, and raises the note that follows it by one semitone:

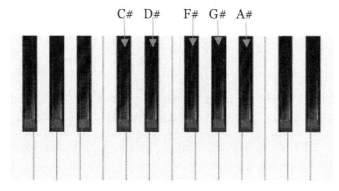

If, at any point in your musical learning, you decide it's funny to call sharps 'hashtags' then get yourself to the circus because you're a fucking clown.

Flats:

A flat sign (♭) is placed before a note on the stave, and lowers the note that follows it by one semitone:

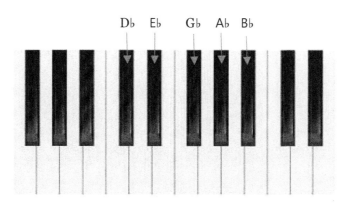

As you can see, the black notes have two different names – one a sharp, one a flat. It's kind of like the difference between UK and American English. Sidewalk versus pavement. Faucet versus tap. Semi-automatic rifles by the bed for home protection versus an extendable umbrella you put somewhere...maybe the boot of the car.

Naturals:

A natural sign (♮) is placed before a note on a stave. It cancels out a previously used sharp or flat in the bar. Usually, this means a black note is changed back to a white note.

Any flat, sharp, or natural used in a bar ceases to have any effect in the bars that follow. Each bar starts afresh, like that singer from the 80s who did something inappropriate with groupie and went into hiding for two decades, then made a comeback by changing his hairstyle and doing some reality TV.

It's time to try out these sharps, flats, and naturals. Unless you've got something better to do, which seems doubtful considering you've chosen to take up the piano to fill the gaping voids in your empty, meaningless life.

1.

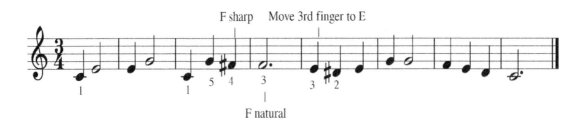

2.

Ƒun Ƒact! Frederic Chopin's heart was pickled in a jar of alcohol and is still encased in a stone pillar in Holy Cross Church, Warsaw.

3.

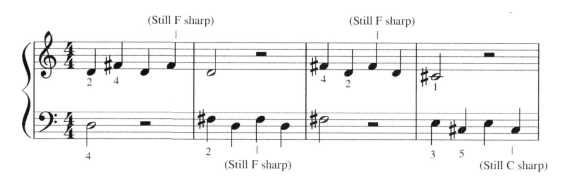

4.

5.

This one *should* sound like a waltz. If it doesn't then you're probably counting incorrectly, which is startling considering all you've got to do is count to three repeatedly.

Scales & Key Signatures.

Johann Sebastian Bach fathered twenty children. This gives us a pretty good idea of how the randy old sod spent a lot of his time pursuing 'horizontal recreation' and (assuming he made a good job of it) how it would've eaten into his composing schedule somewhat. Imagine having to write all those notes down by hand - just you, your quill, and an ice pack for your red-raw junk. Then, on top of that, having to write every single flat, sharp, and natural next to the notes that need them on the score. I'm knackered just thinking about it. Therefore, in an effort to save time, ink, and wear-and-tear on the wrist, key signatures were born.

A **key signature** tells us which notes are to be sharpened or flattened when we encounter them, eliminating the need for each one to be written on the score individually. It appears at the beginning of the music and consequently at the beginning of each line of music. It's equal parts clever and lazy, a bit like a geography teacher in their late fifties just bunging on a video about oxbow lakes every lesson, and counting down the days until retirement when they can use their pension to buy a second hand camper van and drive far, far away from these godawful children.

In order to understand key signatures, we must also understand **scales**.
A scale comprises 8 notes played in order. Major scales always follow this pattern, no matter which letter of the alphabet they start from.

Scale of C Major:

* T = Tone
* st = semitone

To make sure this pattern is maintained, we have to add sharps or flats into our scales where needed.

Scale of G Major:

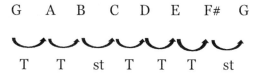

As you can see, the scale of C major has no sharps or flats, therefore a piece of music written in the key of C major (ie. Uses the notes within a C major scale) has no sharps or flats in its key signature:

A piece written in the key of G major would contain a sharp sign on the F line of the stave, since the scale of G major contains an F#:

It's a wonderful system which helps not only the clarity of the score for the piano player, but also probably frees up a lot of shagging time for the composer.

Let's try out a piece with a key signature and see how you get on, shall we? Every F you see is actually an F sharp.

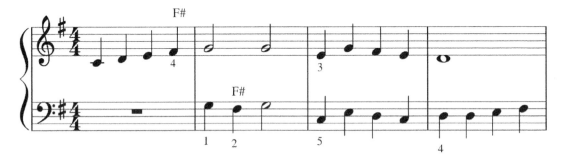

Did you manage it? Do you feel all brainy and arty, now? Or are you silently wondering which co-worker you can palm this book off onto when Secret Santa comes around?

A Bit of General Practise.

If you are eager to learn and improve your knowledge and technique, follow the music carefully, ensure you're in the correct hand position, and count a steady pulse. If you'd prefer to half-arse it, you can guess at a couple of notes before knocking out a shoddy rendition of 'Chopsticks'. Might as well bung more of last night's pizza in the microwave while you're at it, you greasy-fingered loser.

1. (Hand position – C Major.)

2. Hand position – G Major (RH thumb on G, LH little finger on G.)

Fun Fact! Entertainer and composer Ivor Novello was sent to prison for four weeks for misusing petrol coupons.

3.

'Happy Birthday To You.'

Stretch 5 to G

Put 3rd finger over to B

Stretch 5 to F

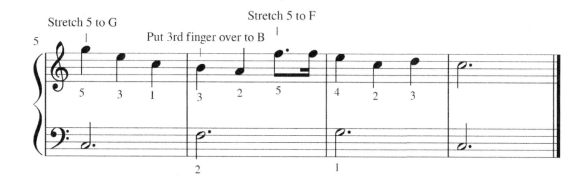

4.

Brahms' Lullaby

Chords.

If you've ever been to a party where some checked-shirt no-socks toe-ring idiot ruins it by getting out his acoustic guitar and playing dull renditions of 90s indie hits, intermittently explaining how he was *this close* to being signed by Gold Douche Records back in the late seventies, then you'll certainly have heard chords.

CHORDS are two or more notes played at the same time.

That's it. That's a chord.
There are varying degrees of difficulty and sophistication when it comes to the structure of chords, but here, we're going to deal with some of the more basic ones to ease you into it. I don't want you running off to your therapist to show them on the doll where the mean piano book hurt you.

Here are some chords of two notes. You should probably play them.

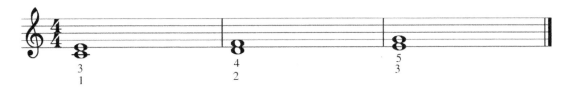

Here are some chords of three notes. Play these, too.

They sound pretty good, don't they? Or at least they should, if you're playing them correctly. If your chords sound like someone with fillings chewing on tinfoil, then something has gone wrong.

ƒun ƒact! Madrigal Master Carlo Gesualdo killed his wife and her lover with a knife. Unsure that they were fully dead, he later returned to the bodies to mutilate them.

Imagine a world where everybody suddenly stops using their words in the correct order. Sentence structure is out of the window.

Instead of the bus driver saying *'That'll be one pound seventy'* she says *'Seventy pound one that'll be.'*

Instead of the telemarketer asking if you'd like *'a quote for new double-glazed windows'*, he asks if you'd like *'Double windows, glazed for a new quote.'*

Instead of your partner asking *'shall we go out for a meal at a nice restaurant tonight?'* they ask *'Are you ever going to wear that sexy lingerie I bought for you, or is it just going to sit in the drawer? You know, I bought that to try and inject some passion back into this relationship but it seems like you're not really trying... Oh, that's right, throw Crystal in my face. That's what all this is about, isn't it? You said we were okay but we're not, that seems pretty clear... you know what? I bet Crystal would wear that lingerie, you're right. But then that's no surprise, is it, because YOU'RE ALWAYS RIGHT.'*

Without structure in our sentences they are nonsense, and unpleasant to listen to. In music, too, we need structure. We're not talking about lingerie in this case (although absolutely nobody is stopping you slipping on a pair of crotchless numbers if it helps you get in the mood for learning) – no, we're talking about chords and the order in which we use them.

Let's go back to our simplest scale – C Major:

I	II	III	IV	V	VI	VII	I
C	D	E	F	G	A	B	C

We're using Roman Numerals to label each note's position in the scale. If you're not comfortable using Roman Numerals, run and fetch your favourite crayon so you can write in the Arabic versions you're used to. Maybe later, after your practice is finished, you can draw a nice picture of your dad's second wife on his midlife-crisis boat. Maybe you can draw her falling overboard. Maybe there's a shark in the water, too. You still hate her, don't you? All of the old feelings are coming flooding back, aren't they? That time he didn't show up to your birthday because he was in the Canary Islands with Sandra. Or that time he was supposed to come watch your school's production of 'Oliver' because you had eleven lines and a dance routine, but he rang at the last minute to say Sandra had a cold so he had to stay home and nurse her, but then the next day you saw them both in WH Smiths and she didn't look sick to you.

But anyway.

Chords.

If we are playing in the key of C Major, we can build chords from each of the notes in that scale:

Chord I would be C-E-G
Chord II would be D-F-A
Chord III would be E-G-B
Chord IV would be F-A-C
Chord V would be G-B-D
Chord VI would be A-C-E
Chord VII would be B-D-F

A chord progression is the order in which we use the chords, and it is as fundamentally important as the order in which we use our words.

The most common chord progression is

I - V - IV - I

What this means is that chord I would be played for a couple of bars, followed by chord V, changing to chord IV, and then coming back to chord I.
In the key of C major, it would look like this:

C-E-G then **G-B-D** then **F-A-C** then **C-E-G**

Of course, there are vastly more complex chord progressions and combinations throughout music, but this is the most basic one. This is the Victoria Sponge of music structure.
A huge number of pop songs are written using this chord formula only, because pop music is for kids and simpletons.

You're going to play a few pieces now that will use this chord progression, and you will hear it for yourself.

1.   Playing chords like this involves moving your hand(s) into different positions as you go along. If you've thrown a lot of gang signs in your life, you'll probably find this quite easy.

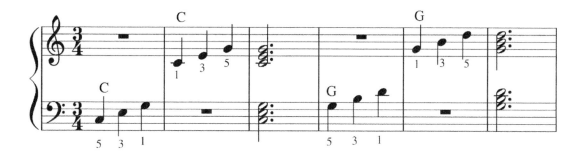

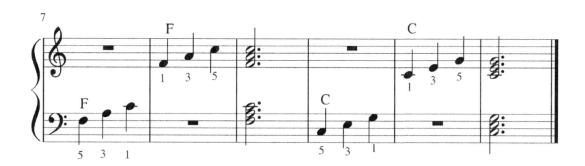

2.

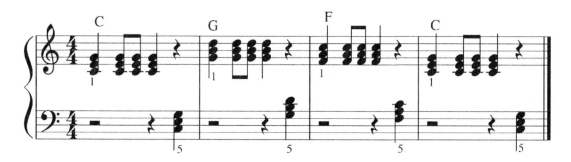

3. Make sure you move your 5th finger to the lowest note of each left hand chord.

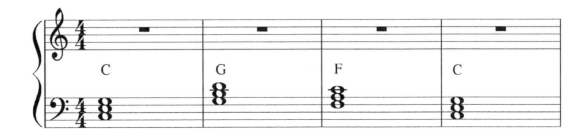

Fun Fact! Mozart, Beethovem, Schumann, Schubert, Hoffman, and Scott Joplin all had syphillis.

4.

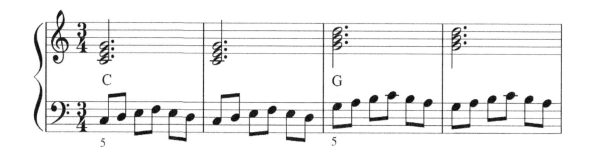

5.   This one begins with your RH 3rd finger on A.

6. These chords are in the key of G Major, so don't forget to play F# instead of F.

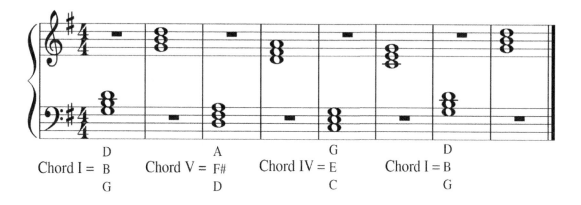

Chord I = D B G   Chord V = A F# D   Chord IV = G E C   Chord I = D B G

7.   Here is a variation on a chord, using the notes F#-C-D.

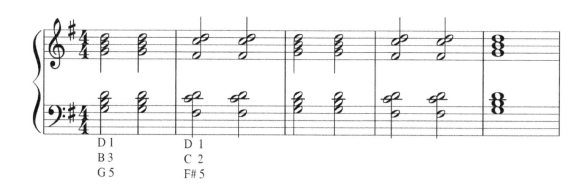

D 1
B 3
G 5

D 1
C 2
F# 5

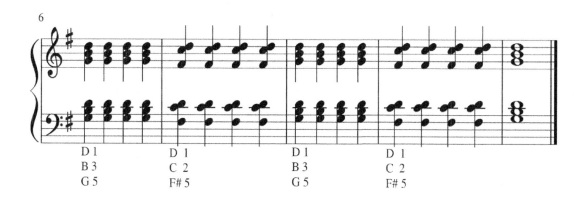

D 1
B 3
G 5

D 1
C 2
F# 5

D 1
B 3
G 5

D 1
C 2
F# 5

8. The melody (main tune) in this piece is in the LH. Make the RH quieter so that the melody comes through clearly.

F sharp

Expression.

Picture the dullest person you know. Now imagine that they have you cornered in a lift. You can't get away, and they've just started telling you about a recent change of bus route that has added an extra six and a half minutes onto their daily commute. The story is detailed – oh, so detailed – and their voice is slow and monotone. There are eleven more floors to go. They're telling you the bus's previous route, with every stop between their house and work (there are a lot of stops) and then they're going to tell you about the changes to that route and some of the new stops that have been incorporated into it.

Are you dying inside? Do you wish you didn't have ears? This is what boring people to do other people, and it's what we want to avoid when we play music.

Expression in music is what gives it its life. The loud parts, the soft parts, the harsh parts, the smooth parts. Without expression, music is a one-sided conversation about a change of bus route.

Since it was the Italians who first wrote directions on the music for performers, Italian has become the main language we still use for this purpose today.

forte = loud
mf (mezzo forte) = Moderately loud
fortissimo = very loud

piano = soft
mp (mezzo piano) = Moderately soft
pianissimo = very soft

Crescendo = gradually getting louder

Decrescendo = gradually getting softer

Staccato = dots that tell the performer to play the notes short and detached

Legato = curved lines that tell the performer to play the notes smoothly

Let's play these two identical pieces of music in two completely different ways.

1. Every note with a dot should be played 'staccato.'

2. The notes with curved lines should be played 'legato'.

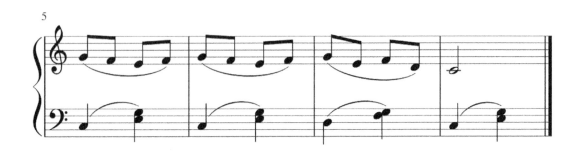

Here we have a piece to play through twice. The first time it will be fast ('allegro') and loud ('forte') and the second time it will be slow ('adagio') and soft ('piano'.)

When applying expression to a piece of music, it's often useful to get yourself into the right mindset by thinking of a feeling. For example, when playing a loud, fast piece you could imagine yourself taking a sledgehammer to your neighbour's stereo, the one that plays godawful club music that goes DMPH-DMPH-DMPH through the wall. Or you could imagine how it would feel to chase your neighbour down the road with that sledgehammer because two a.m. is never an acceptable time to play loud club music, especially on a weeknight.

When playing soft, gentle music, you could think about how lovely and quiet it is now that your neighbour has moved away into witness protection.

'Ties' – when two notes are tied together, we simply add one to the other and play as one continuous note. In this piece, a minim is tied to a crotchet, which gives us 3 beats to count. In order for two notes to be tied together, they must be of the same pitch.

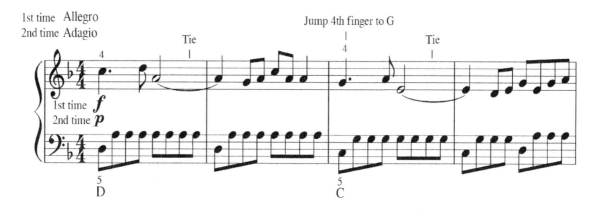

Fun Fact! After a heavy night out on the town, Henry Purcell's wife locked him out of the house. He contracted pneumonia and later died.

Major and Minor Keys.

There are many technical differences between major and minor keys, but this is a book for beginners and day-drinkers, so I'll keep it basic;

Music written in a Major key tends to sound happy, joyful, and sweet, like an art teacher with oversized necklaces and a faint whiff of patchouli.

Music written in a minor key tends to sound ominous, serious, and spooky, like a Goth tax inspector.

With this in mind, we can change the whole feel of a piece of music by switching it from major to minor, and vice versa.

The following two exercises are almost identical except for the addition in the second of an accidental that changes the sound from Major to minor:

1.

2.

Pieces.

If you have read and practiced each page carefully mindfully, then you are ready for this section. If you used this book as a coaster for your tea whilst you watched The Real Girlfriends of Plastic County, then please enjoy the colouring-in at the end instead, you flaky twat.

This one is adapted from *Beethoven's Ninth Symphony*. Beethoven was deaf for much of his life, yet he still managed to knock out some incredible, moving compositions, most of which we still recognise and enjoy today. What a legacy.

Don't feel intimidated by this, though – I'm sure your regularly pressure-washed driveway will ensure you're remembered for at least a few weeks after your death.

Minuet in G Major
JS Bach

46

D.C al Fine stands for 'Da Capo al Fine'. 'Da Capo' means 'from the top/beginning' whilst 'fine' means 'the end.' Therefore, when you get to the bottom of this piece, you are instructed to go back to the beginning and play to the 'fine' in order to finish.

Swan Lake
Tchaikovsky

As promised on page 45, here is a potato for you to colour in. Try not to fuck it up.

You did it!

Well, who'd'a thunk it? You did it! You started this book, didn't give up, and now look at you – you've accomplished something! You're *reading* music. You're *playing* music. You're *understanding* music.

Sarcasm aside, I'm really proud of you for doing this. Playing the piano isn't easy, and learning it step-by-step is often frustrating. It's all too easy to give up and go watch some crappy soap opera instead, but you didn't do that. You persevered.

So where do you go from here?

Firstly, you need to brag. Maybe post about it on social media, along with a photo of you sitting at the piano with the caption 'Look at me, I'm Elton Liberace!' or something. Fuck being humble. Go brag. Go on! Go!

Secondly, you must carry on playing the piano. Don't stop now. Find pieces you like the sound of, and learn them. Play slowly, make mistakes, practice them out until you have a whole stack of music you can play for your own amusement or on those cronky old pianos at train stations. It sounds clichéd but practice really does make perfect, and if it doesn't make perfect, it certainly makes improvements.

Have cake for dinner tonight.

You deserve it.

About the author.

L. Blake has been teaching children and adults how to play the piano since 1998. In the beginning, her heart was full of joy and hope for her students, for music, and for the future.

However, much like a leaking sewage pipe, all positivity has slowly seeped away over time until all that is left is an empty tube that smells of disappointment.

L. Blake 2020

Printed in Great Britain
by Amazon